50 Classical Guitar Solos

in Tablature

REVISED EDITION

Arranged by

Howard Wallach

CONTENTS

Acquisition and editorial: Nathaniel Gunod
Cover : Timothy Phelps
Cover photo of Hauser guitar courtesy of Guitar Salon International

ISBN 1-929395-13-2

Signs, Symbols and Terms
Used in this Book

Right Hand Indications

p - Thumb
i - Index Finger
m - Middle Finger
a - Ring Finger
↑ - Arpeggiate the chord with right-hand
   fingers or thumb

Left Hand Indications

⌣ or ⌣ or ⌢ or ⌢ - Hammer-on if to a higher note, or pull-off if to a lower note.

B or C - Bar indicated fret with 1st finger.

½B or ½C - Half bar indicated fret.

♯ = *Sharp*. Raise the note one half step (one fret).

𝄪 = *Double Sharp*. Raise the note one whole step (two frets).

♭ = *Flat*. Lower the note one half step (one fret).

♭♭ = *Double flat*. Lower the note one whole step (two frets).

♮ = Natural. Returns a sharp or flat to its natural position.

⑥ = D - Tune the 6th string down to D
⑤ = G - Tune the 6th string down to G
③ = F♯ - Tune the 3rd string down to F♯

$\frac{2}{4}$ $\frac{3}{4}$ $\frac{4}{4}$ $\frac{6}{8}$ C ¢ = *Time Signatures*. The number on top indicates the number of beats per measure. The number on the bottom indicates which note value equals one beat. A "4" indicates that the quarter note equals one beat. An "8" indicates that the eighth note equals one beat. The C refers to *common time*, which is the same as $\frac{4}{4}$ time. The ¢ refers to *cut time*, which is the same as $\frac{2}{2}$ time.

⌐1.¬ ⌐2.¬ = *1st and 2nd endings*. Play ⌐1.¬ the first time; play ⌐2.¬ the second time, omitting ⌐1.¬.

‖: :‖ = *Repeat signs*.

D.C. al Fine = *Da Capo al Fine*. Repeat from the beginning until the word **Fine** (end).

⌒ = *Fermata*. Hold sign. Indicates that the note should be held for longer than its written duration.

⌣ or ⌢ = *Tie*. Joins two or more notes of the same pitch to create one longer note that lasts for the duration of the combined note values.

Tempo Indications

Adagio — Slowly; smoothly, leisurely.
Allegretto — Quite lively; moderately fast, between **Andante** and **Allegro**.
Allegro — Lively; fast, brisk, rapid.
Andante — Moving at a moderate rate.
Andantino — A little slower than **Andante**, but often used as if meaning a little faster.
Larghetto — Slightly faster than **Largo**.
Largo — Very slow; slower than **Adagio**.
Lento — Slow; between **Andante** and **Largo**.
Moderato — **Moderately**; at a moderate rate.

Types of Pieces

Bourrée — 17th and 18th-century French dance in quick $\frac{4}{4}$ time.
Gagliarda/Galliard — 16th-century dance in moderately quick *triple time* (any time signature with three beats to the measure).
Gavotte — 17th and 18th-century French dance in moderate $\frac{4}{4}$ time.
Menuet/Minuet — Graceful dance in moderate triple time.
Pavane — Courtly 16th-century dance in rather slow duple meter (any time signature with two beats to the measure).
Passamezze — 16th-century Italian dance in moderate $\frac{4}{4}$ time.
Prelude — A non - dance piece, sometimes of an introductory character.
Saltarello — 16th-century Italian dance in fast triple meter.
Sarabande — 17th and 18th-century dance in slow triple meter and of a dignified character.
Siciliana — A piece in $\frac{6}{8}$ time or $\frac{12}{8}$ meter in moderate tempo suggestive of a pastoral scene.

Tablature Explanation

Tablature is a system of notation that graphically represents the strings and frets of the guitar fingerboard. Each note is indicated by placing a number, which indicates the fret to play, on the appropriate string.

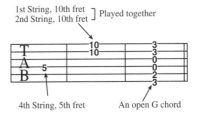

The Arranger

Howard Wallach was born in Cleveland, Ohio. At the age of ten, he began performing on both jazz and classical guitar. After studying with guitar virtuoso Miguel Rubio at the Conservatory of Lausanne, Switzerland, he completed his Bachelor of Music at the Peabody Conservatory of the Johns Hopkins University under the renowned educator Aaron Shearer. His graduate studies were undertaken at the University of Houston.

Mr. Wallach has given many solo and ensemble performances on both guitar and lute in Switzerland, Baltimore, Houston, Washington., D.C., Cleveland and Philadelphia. Currently residing in Houston, he teaches at Houston Community College and at Lee College in Baytown, Texas.

Danza

ANON (16th Century)

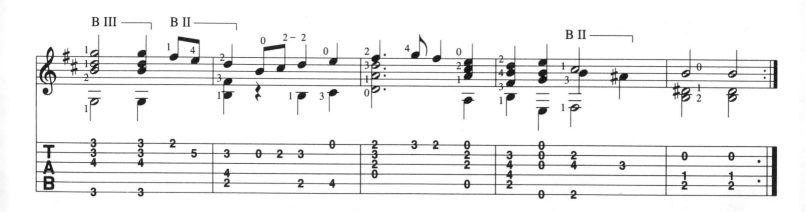

Saltarello

Vincenzo Galilei
(1520 - 1591)

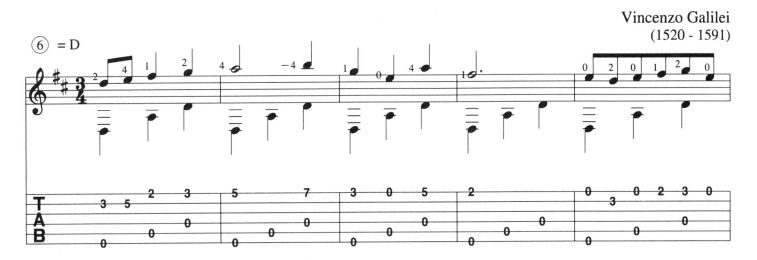

Gagliarda

ANON (16th Century)

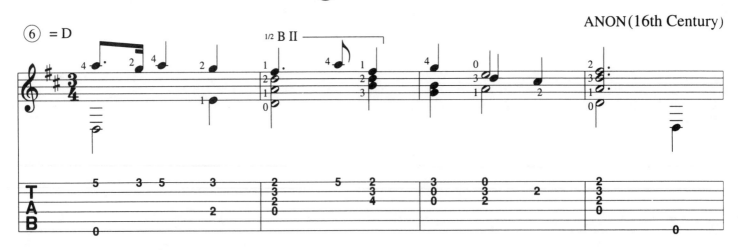

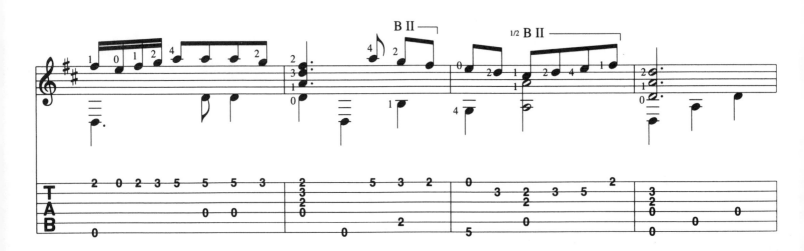

Pavane

Pierre Attaingnant
(c. 1480 - d. 1552)

Galliarde

Pierre Attaingnant
(c. 1480 - d. 1552)

La Brosse

Pierre Attaingmant
(c. 1480 - d. 1552)

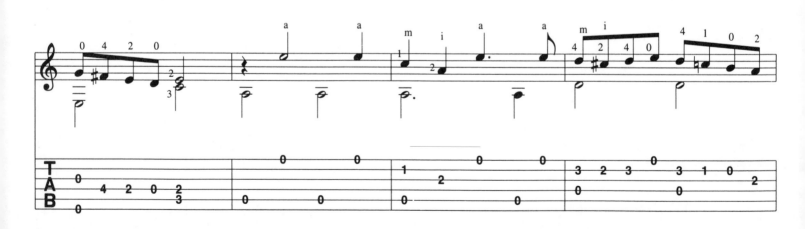

Packington's Pound

Francis Cutting
(16th Century)

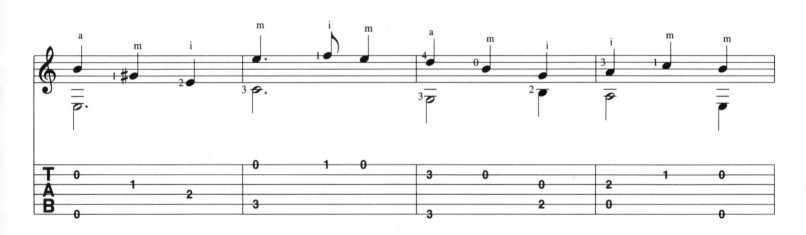

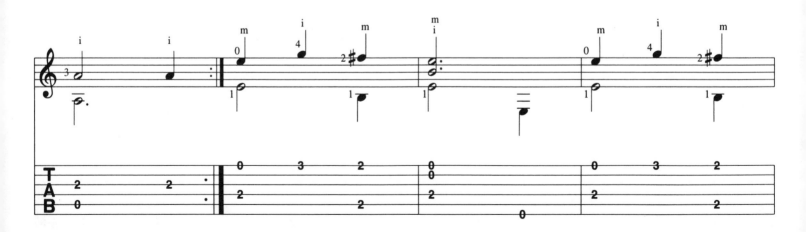

O' Sweet Oliver

ANON (16th Century)

Peg - A - Ramsey

ANON (16th Century)

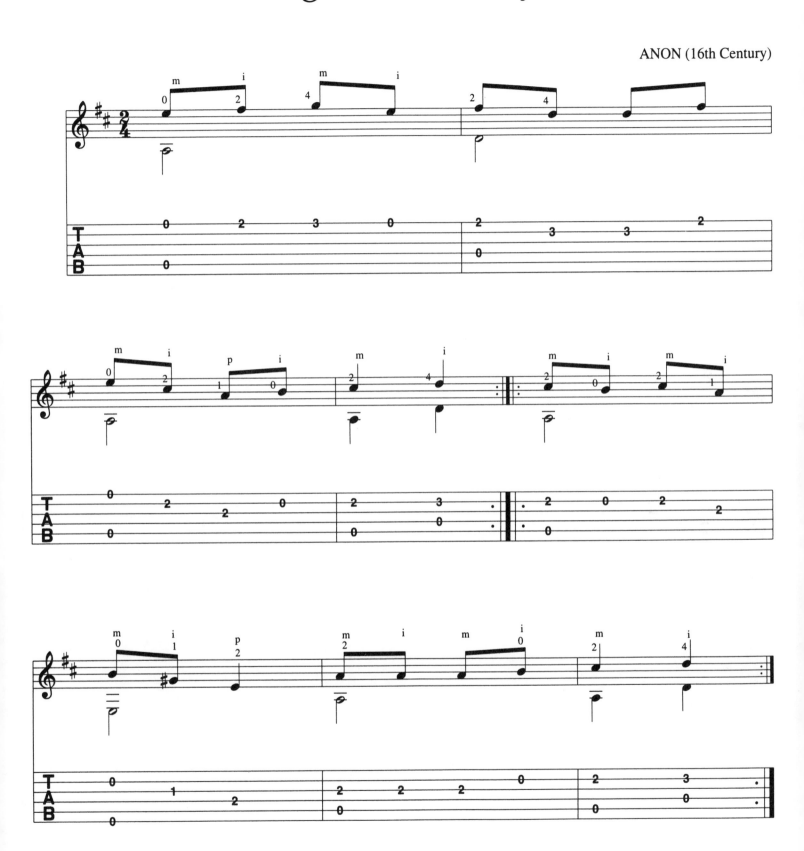

Wilson's Wilde

ANON (16th Century)

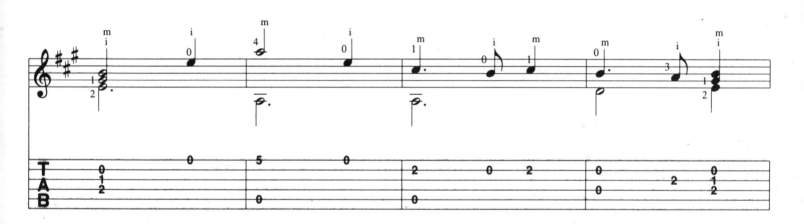

Greensleeves

ANON
Arrangement by H. Wallach

Kemp's Jig

ANON (16th Century)

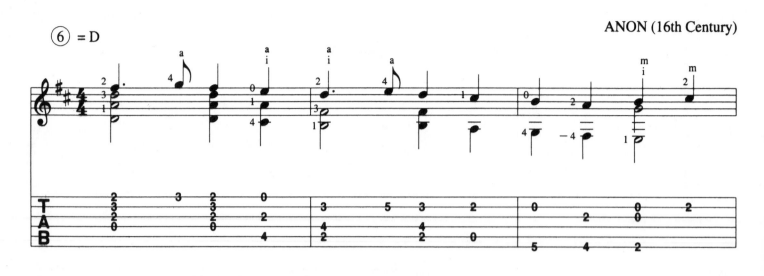

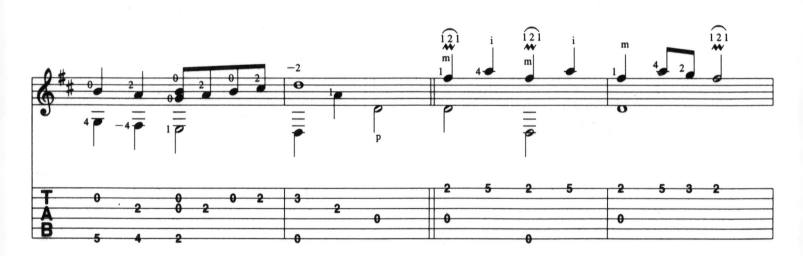

Watkin's Ale

ANON (16th Century)

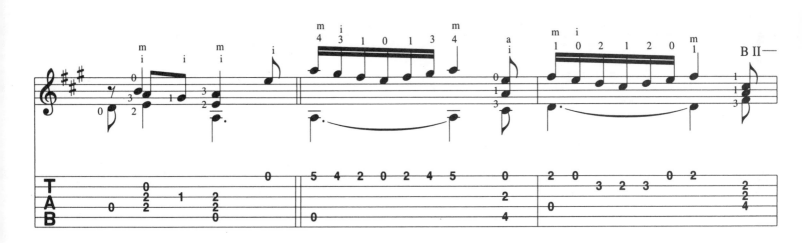

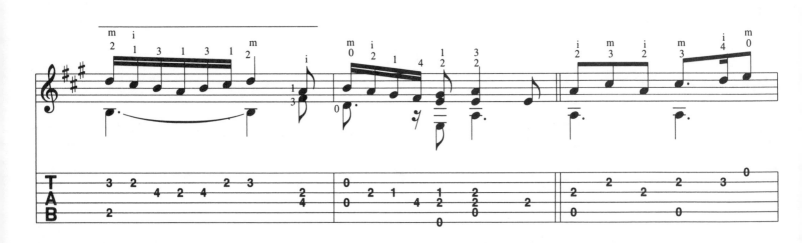

Passamezze

Adrian LeRoy
(1520 - 1598)

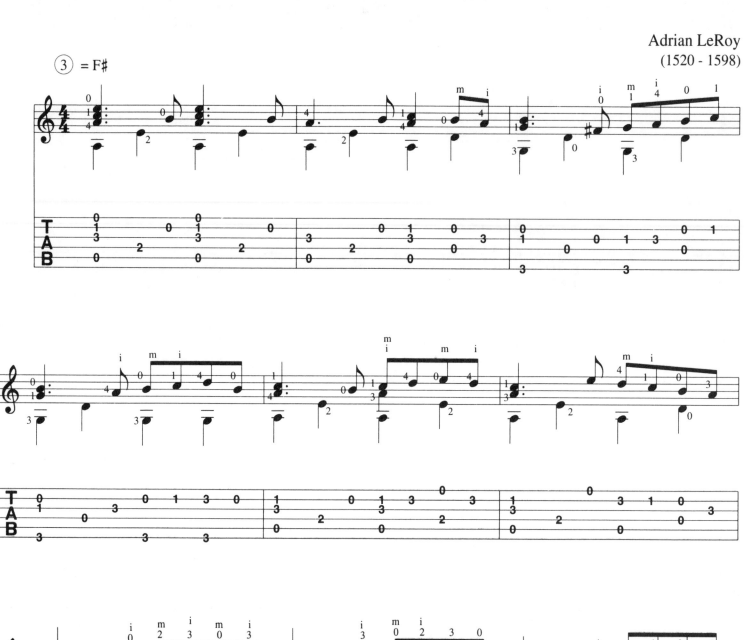

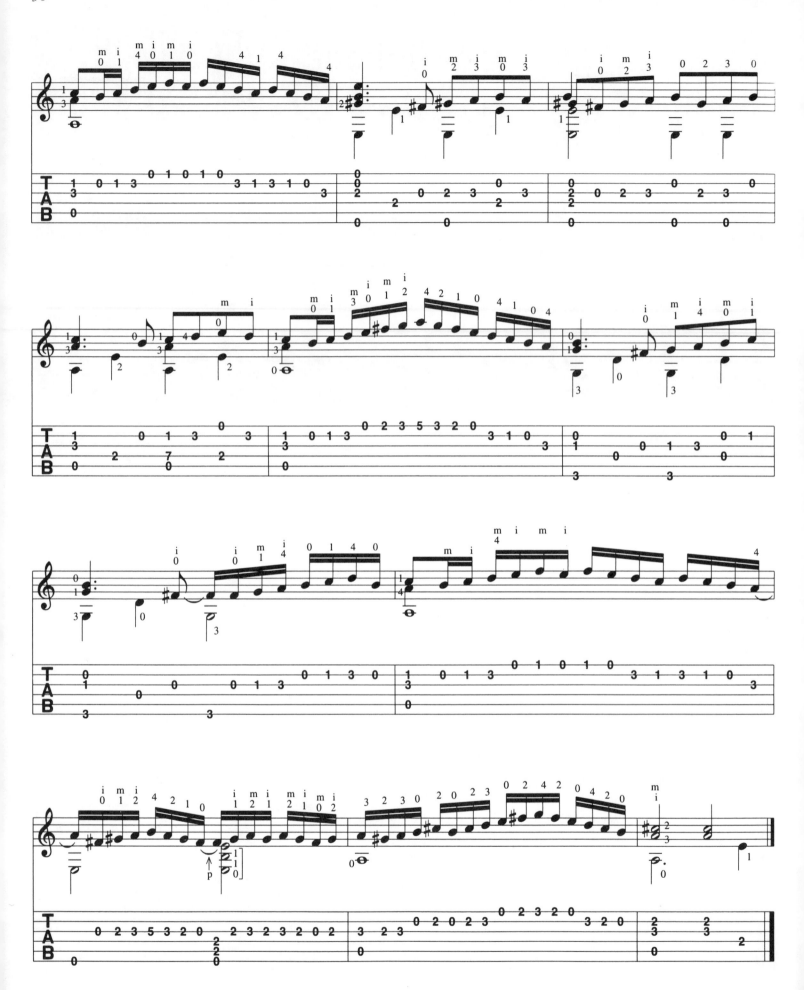

Tordiglione

Carlo Calvi
(c. 1610 - c. 1670)

Spagnoletta

Carlo Calvi
(c. 1610 - c. 1670)

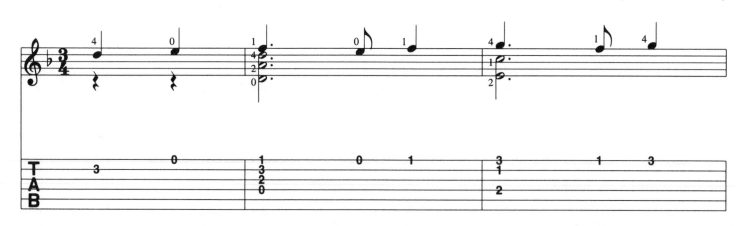

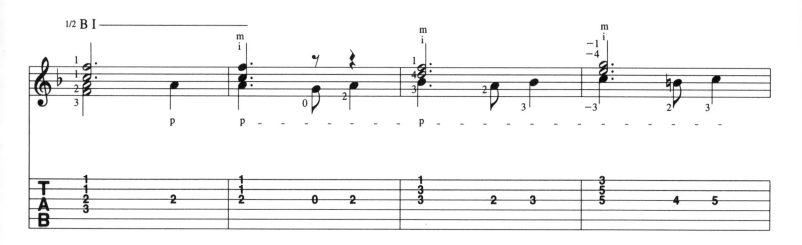

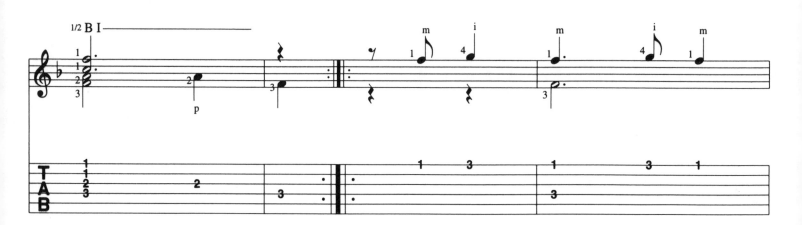

Aria di Fiorenza

Carlo Calvi
(c. 1610 - c. 1670)

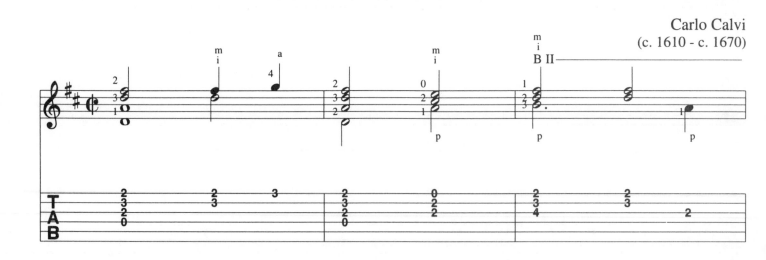

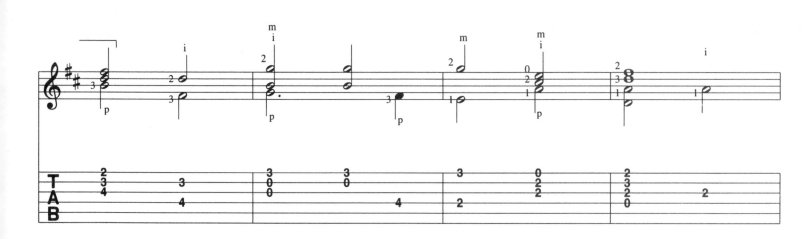

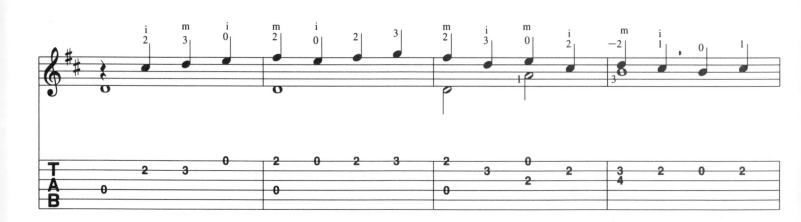

Canario

Carlo Calvi
(c. 1610 - c. 1670)

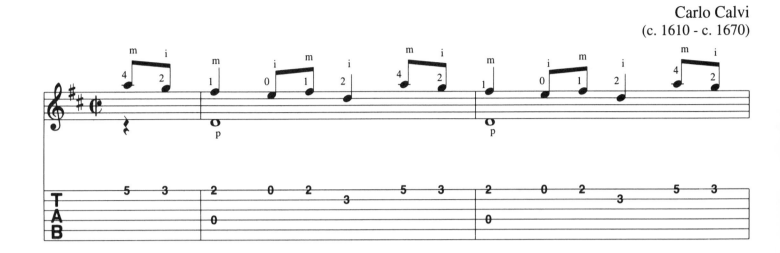

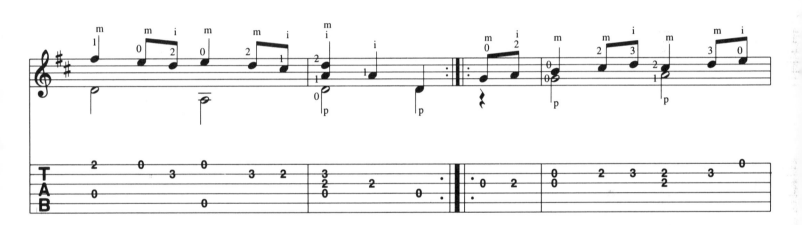

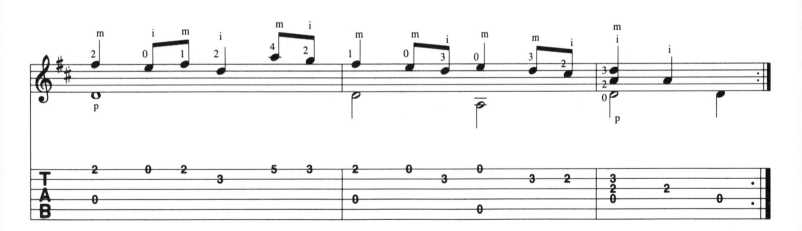

Villano

Gaspar Sanz
(1640 - 1710)

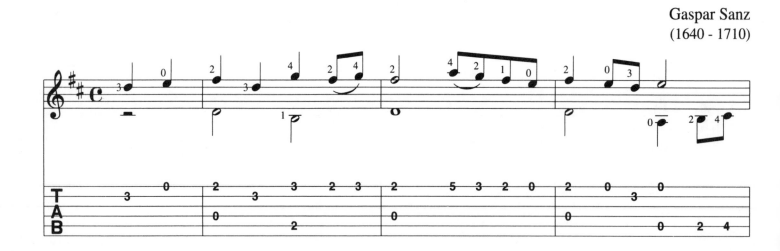

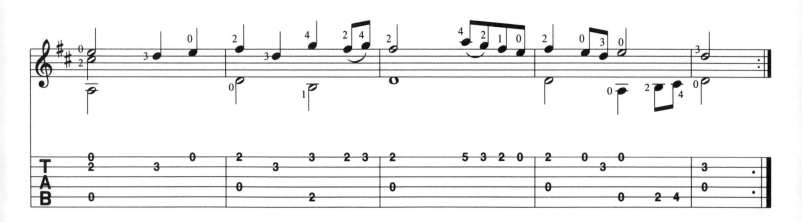

Rujero

Gaspar Sanz
(1640 - 1710)

Españoleta

Gaspar Sanz
(1640 - 1710)

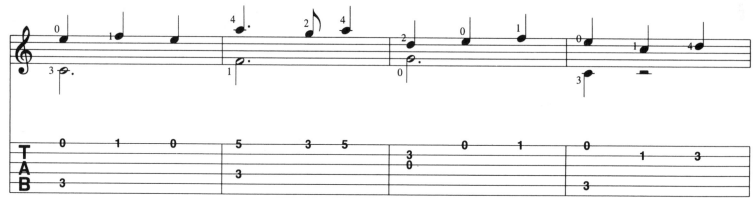

Canarios

Gaspar Sanz
(1640 - 1710)

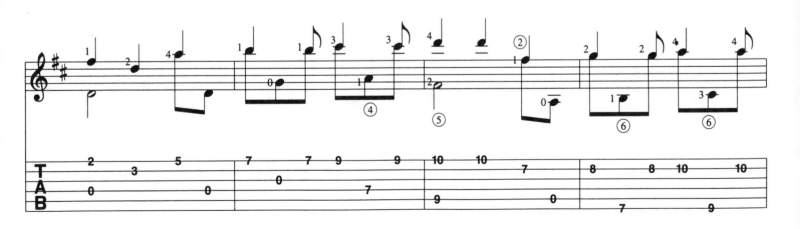

Menuet

Robert de Visée
(c. 1650 - c. 1725)

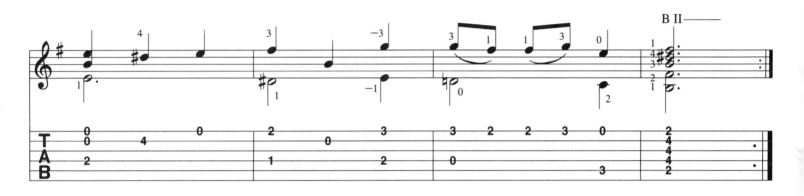

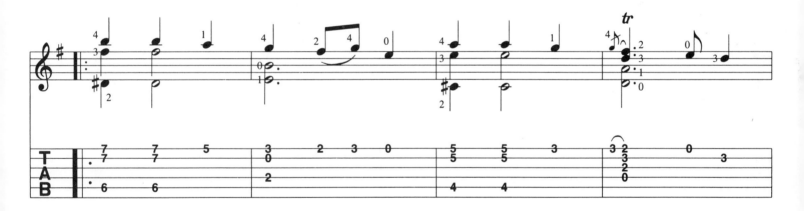

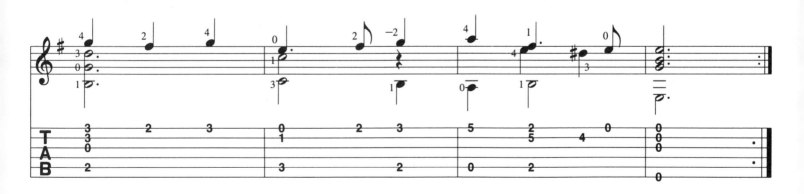

Gavotte

Robert de Visée
(c. 1650 - c. 1725)

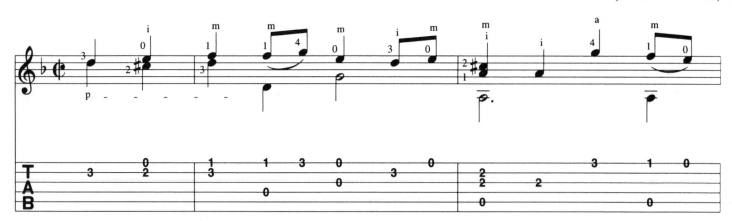

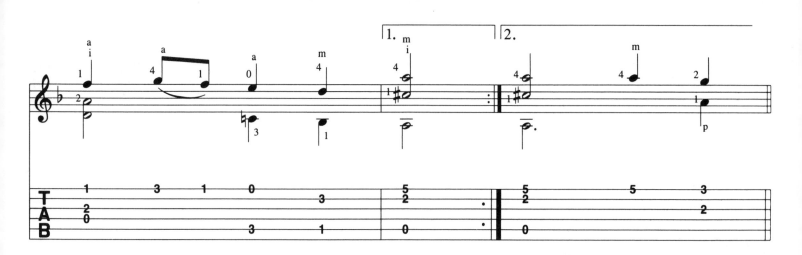

Menuet I

Robert de Visée
(c. 1650 - c. 1725)

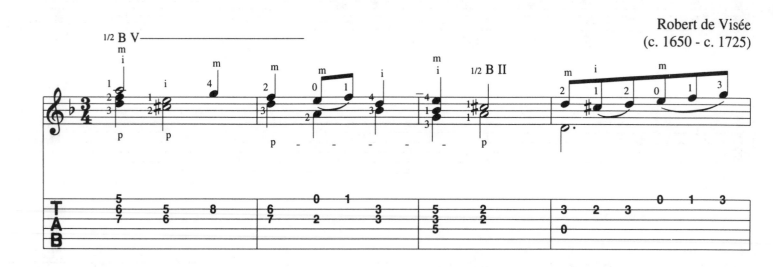

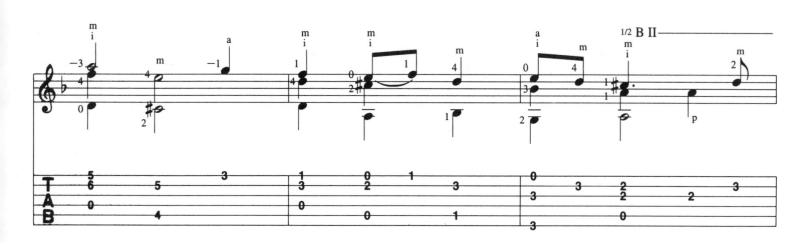

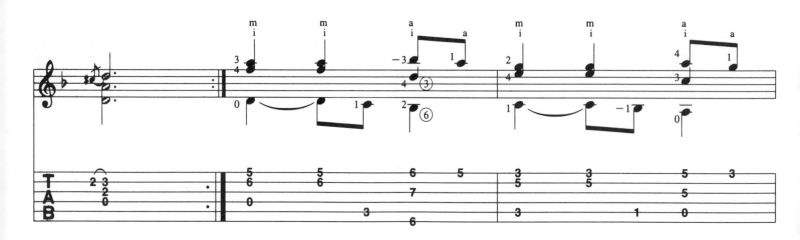

Menuet II

Robert de Visée
(c.1650 - c.1725)

Sarabande

Robert de Visée
(c. 1650 - c. 1725)

Bourrée

Robert de Visée
(c. 1650 - c. 1725)

Prelude in C Major

Matteo Carcassi
(1792 - 1853)

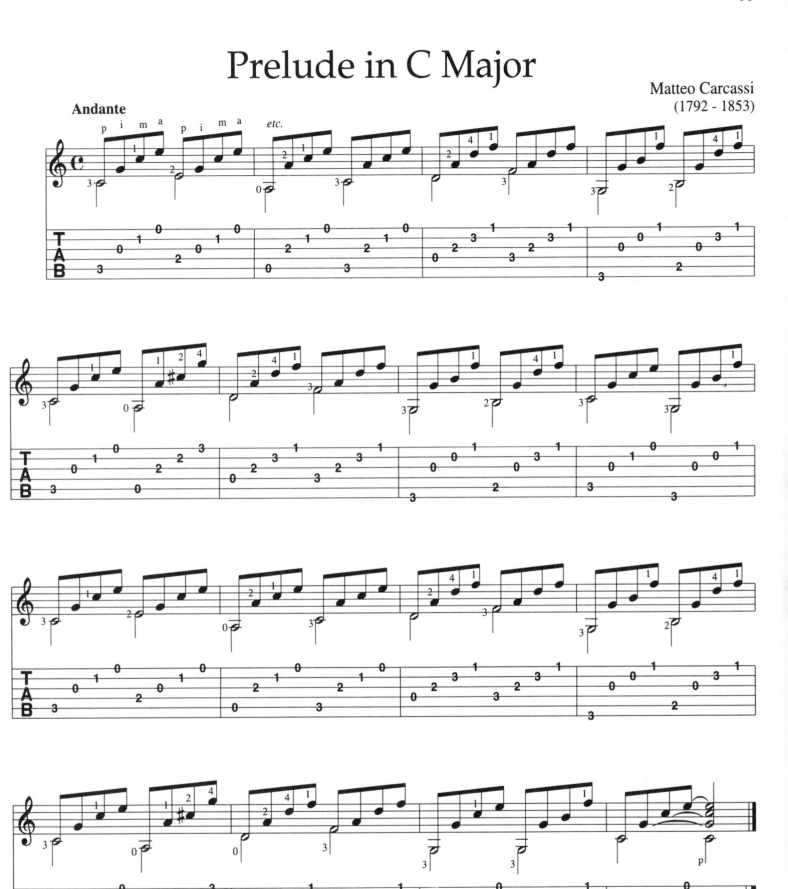

English Dance

Ferdinando Carulli
(1770 - 1841)

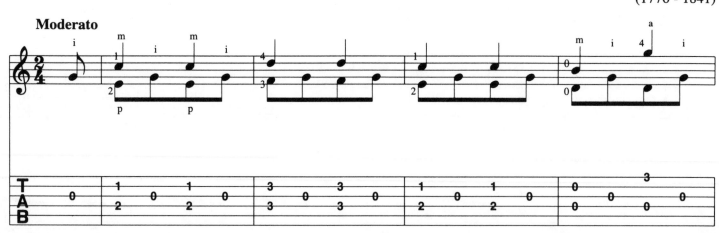

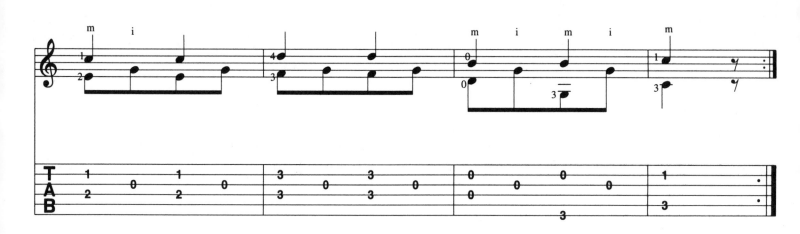

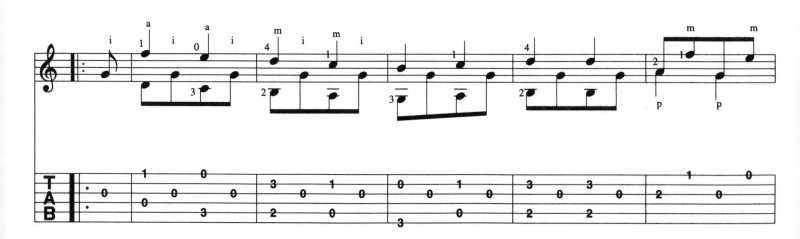

Waltz

Ferdinando Carulli
(1770 - 1841)

D.C. al Fine

Siciliana

Ferdinando Carulli
(1770 - 1841)

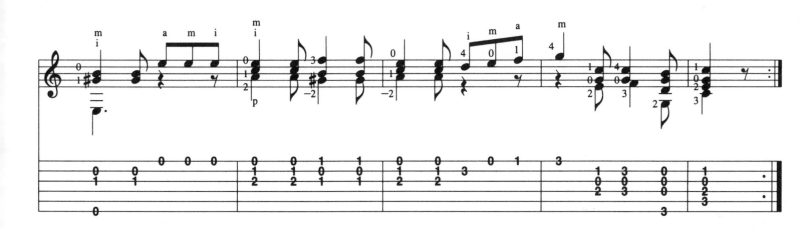

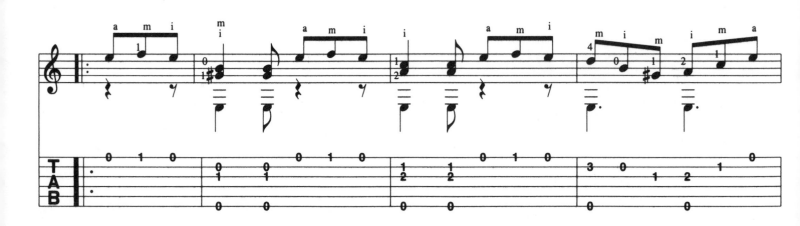

Andantino

Matteo Carcassi
(1792 - 1853)

Study in A Minor

Matteo Carcassi
(1792 - 1853)

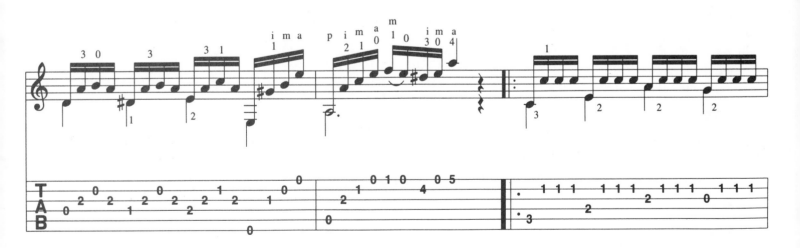

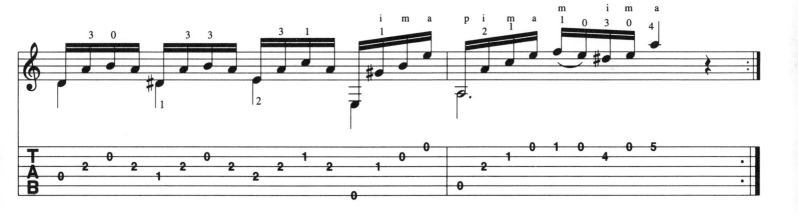

Study in E Minor

Matteo Carcassi
(1792 - 1853)

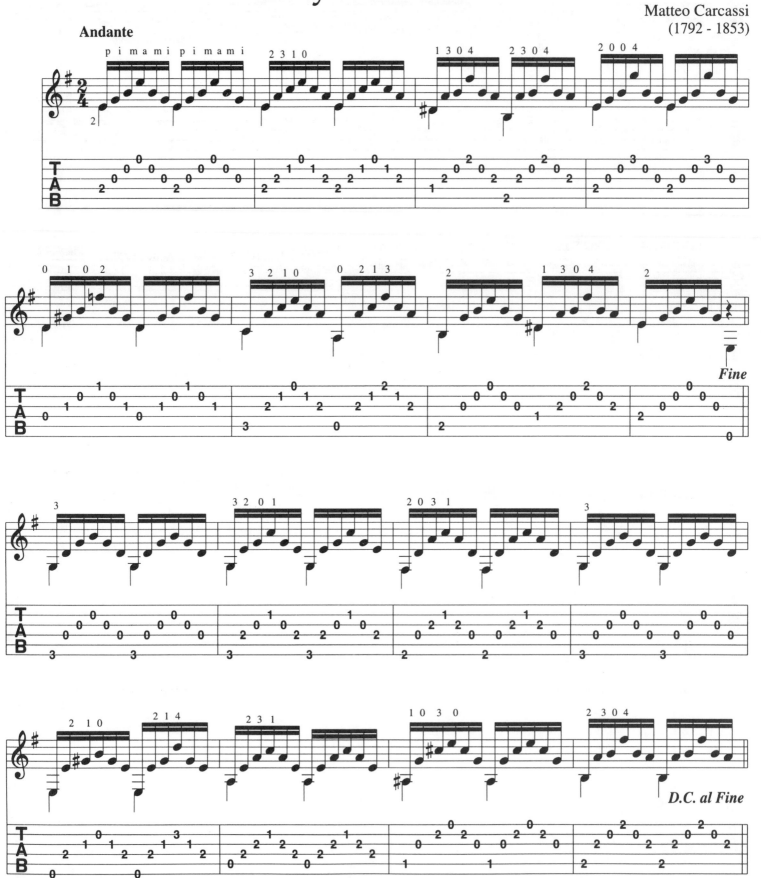

Study in A Minor

Dionisio Aguado
(1784 - 1849)

Study in E Minor

Dionisio Aguado
(1784 - 1849)

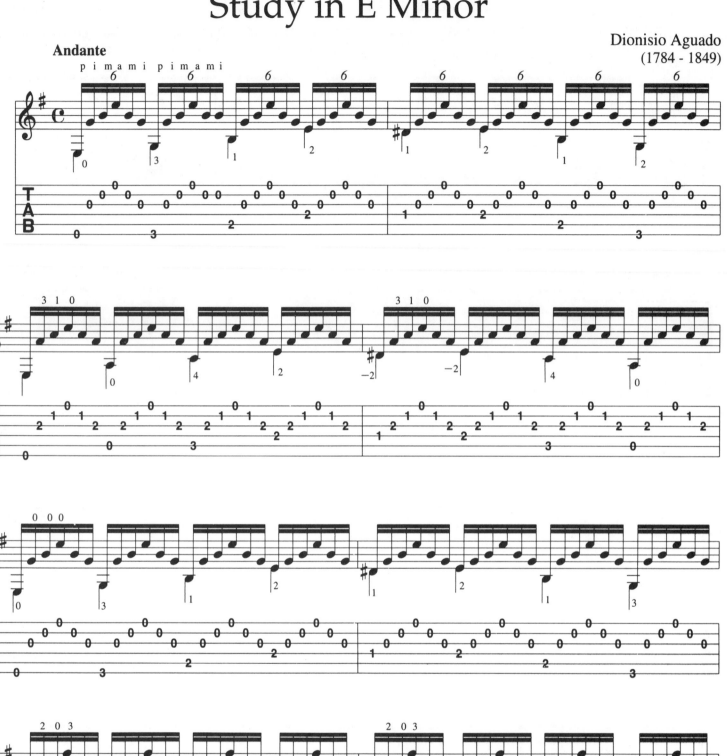

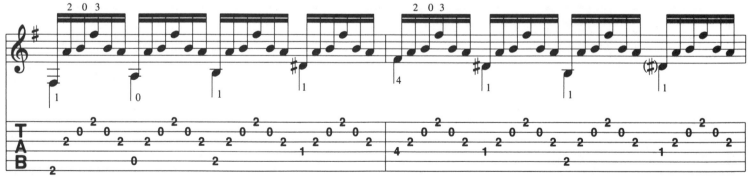

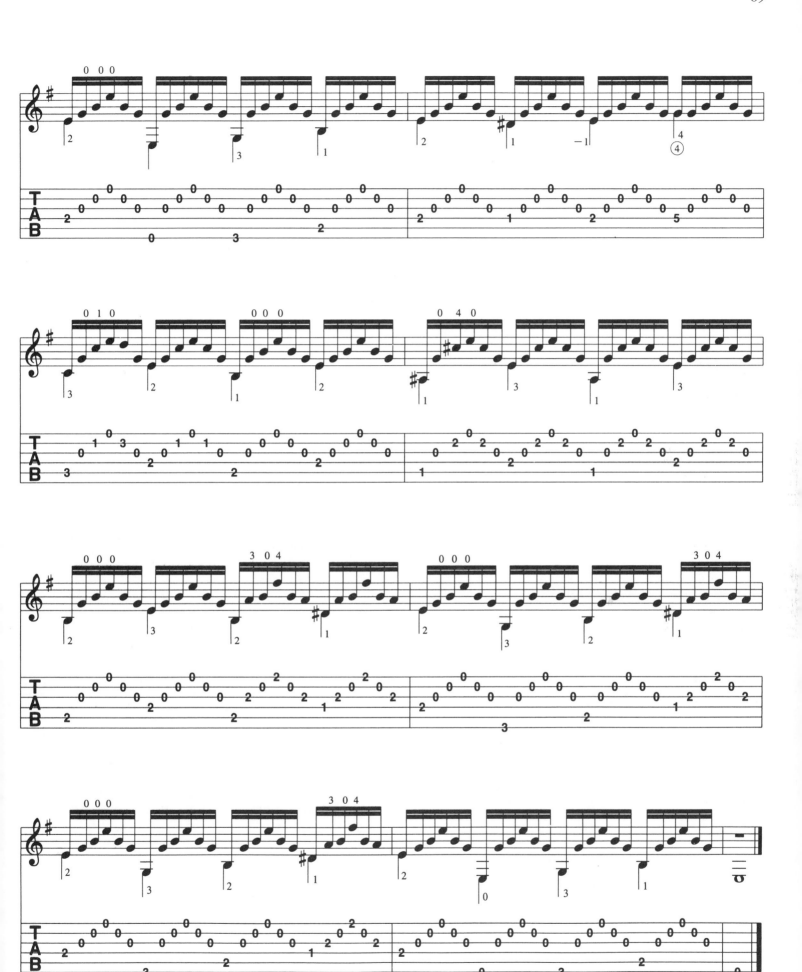

Andante in C Major

Fernando Sor
(1778 - 1839)

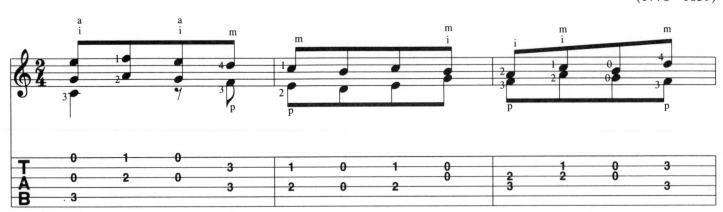

Study in A Minor

Fernando Sor
(1778 - 1839)

Minuet in G Major

Fernando Sor
(1778 - 1839)

Study in A Minor

Fernando Sor
(1778 - 1839)

Andante in E Minor

Fernando Sor
(1778 - 1839)

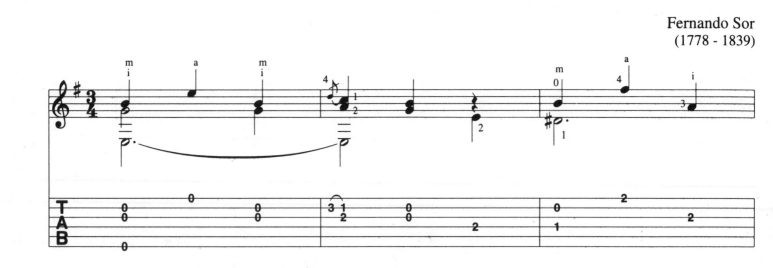

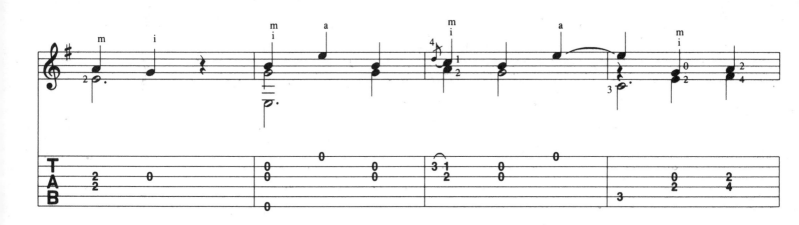

Study in C Major

Fernando Sor
(1780 - 1839)

Study in B Minor

Fernando Sor
(1778 - 1839)

Lagrima

Francisco Tárrega
(1852 - 1909)

Study in C Major

Francisco Tárrega
(1852 - 1909)

Adelita

Francisco Tárrega
(1852 - 1909)

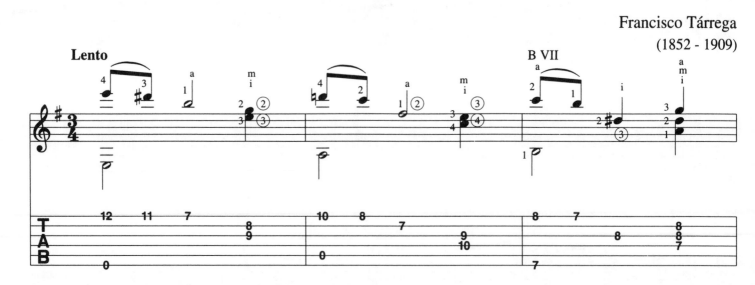

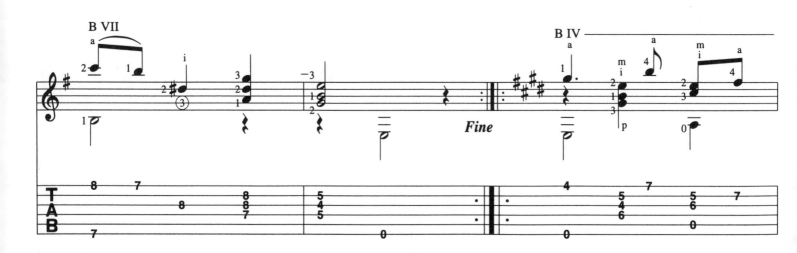

El Noy de la Mare

Traditional Catalan Melody
Arrangement by H. Wallach

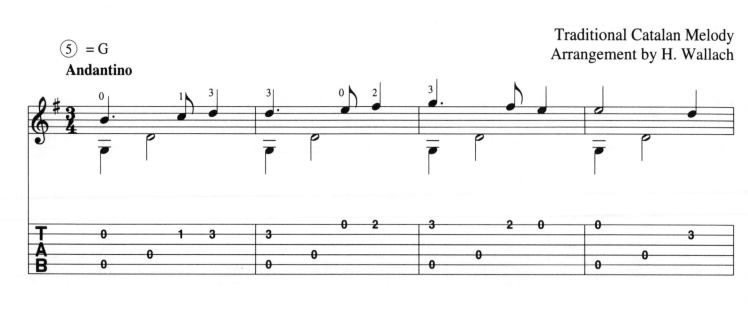

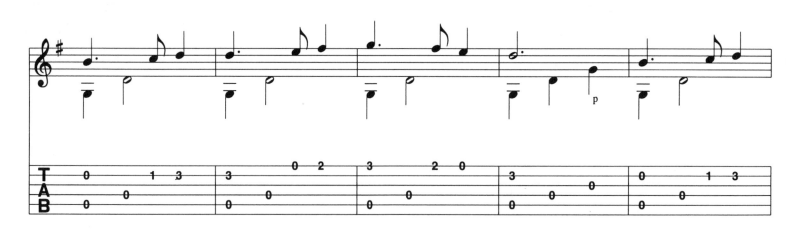

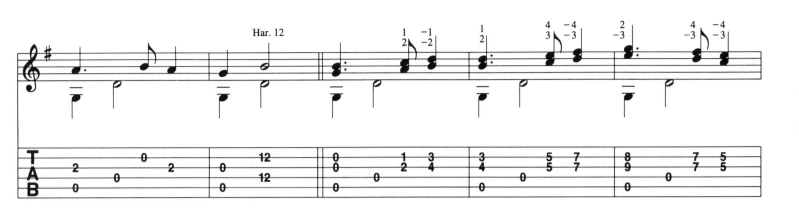

Romance de Amor
(Spanish Ballad)

Traditional
Arrangement by H. Wallach

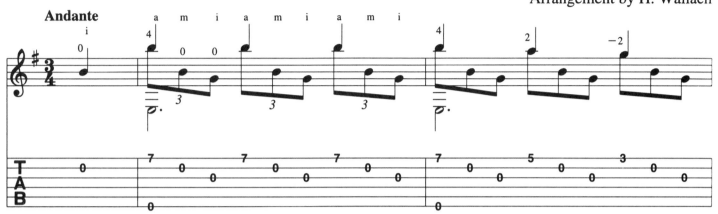

Romance de Amor
Tremolo Version

Howard Wallach

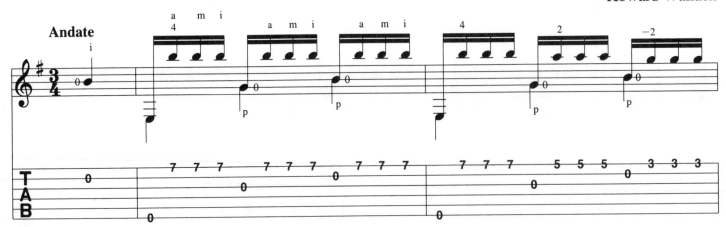

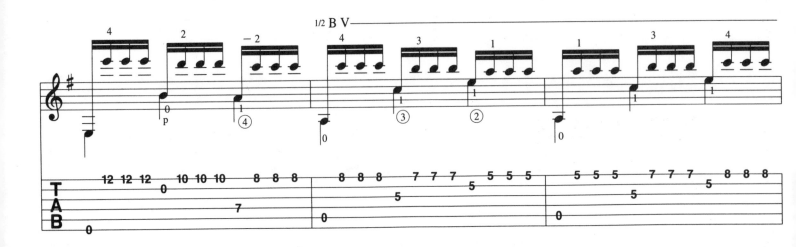